# Mary Lou AND THE Queen Mary 2

**Joan J. Curley**

ILLUSTRATED BY SHANNON D. SCHULTZ

MARY LOU AND THE QUEEN MARY 2
Published by Joan J. Curley
Printed in the U.S.A.

© 2015 Joan J. Curley
All rights reserved

Cover design and interior layout by www.PearCreative.ca
Illustrations by Shannon Schultz | shanzart@hotmail.com

Print ISBN: 978-0-9969365-0-7
eBook ISBN: 978-0-9969365-1-4

This book is dedicated to:

My beloved husband, Neil, who has shared many adventures
with me on the QM2 voyages.

And to:

Charlotte, my affectionately adopted English daughter and Don, her terrific husband,
who live just outside of Southampton, England with the view of
all of the Queens docked in the harbor.

.

# Author's Note

I decided to write this story for young people because I believe that a sense of adventure is a healthy part of growing up. Inquiry into travel, if only by reading a book, is good for the mind. It makes a child aware of other places and activities.

Travel by ship is a good way for families to experience other locations and cultures. The sense of adventure thrives on a ship. There are many things to explore on board as well as on land when visiting different ports.

I used the setting of the Queen Mary 2 because of the different destinations and the marvelous decorative interior and superior facilities.

I try to encourage story book reading as a learning process for young children. I believe this exposure to books challenges them to dream, visualize and explore their thoughts and ideas.

Joan J. Curley<br>
Author

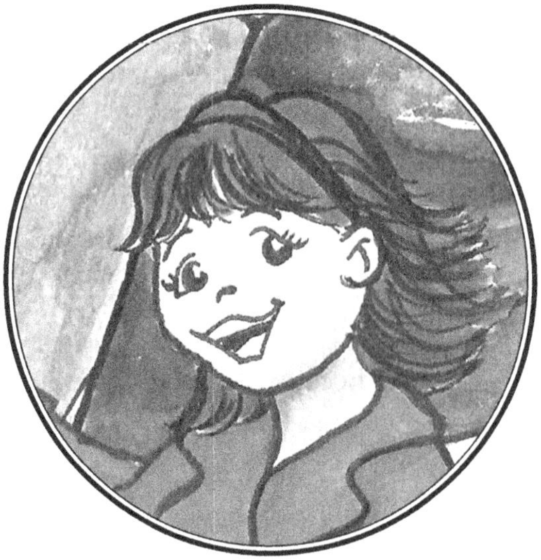

# Introduction of Mary Lou

Hi! My name is Mary Lou. I live in a little village outside the city of London, England.

Over the last few years I have visited my Aunt Charlotte and Uncle Don for a week. They have a house in Hythe Marina Village in Southampton, England.

From their kitchen window I can see the ships as they dock in the port of Southampton. The cruise liners of the Cunard Line are the most distinctive ships with their black and red marking. They are named Queen Elizabeth, Queen Victoria, and the largest of them all, Queen Mary 2.

My Aunt and Uncle own two boats. They are kept at the bottom step of their garden. The garden grows to the water where there is a floating walkway. The larger boat is a pontoon-type boat with sails and an engine for long cruises. The smaller sailboat is used for daily cruises in the harbor. It has an outboard engine to use if we find ourselves becalmed.

I am so very lucky that they have boats! They take me out sailing to see the cruise liners when they are docked. As I gaze upon the big black ships with the red chimneys, I wonder what it is like to sail on those Cunard Line ships. They are called the big ocean liners.

When Aunt Charlotte and Uncle Don are busy, I sit in their yard and stare at those beautiful ships. I think to myself that one day I shall sail on the Queen Mary 2, the largest ship of the three Queens.

Mary Lou begins to daydream about sailing on the Queen Mary 2 cruising to many new places.

She dreams of what the inside of the ship looks like. She wonders if it is like a big grand hotel with a large lobby and a fine dining room with special dressed waiters. She wonders if you take the elevator. Maybe the ship has moving stairs to get to your room like the grand hotels in London. Those stairs are referred to as an escalator.

Mary Lou's thoughts are interrupted when her Aunt Charlotte calls her to come in for lunch. Her Aunt asks why she keeps her eyes on the ships docked across the harbor.

Mary Lou tells her Aunt that she hopes to take a cruise on the Queen Mary 2 someday. She would like to sail to some interesting new places.

Uncle Don heard the conversation and said he had to go to town tomorrow. He would be happy to take Aunt Charlotte and Mary Lou to the local travel agent's shop. He thought Mary Lou could select some travel pamphlets about the Queen Mary 2 and its cruise routes.

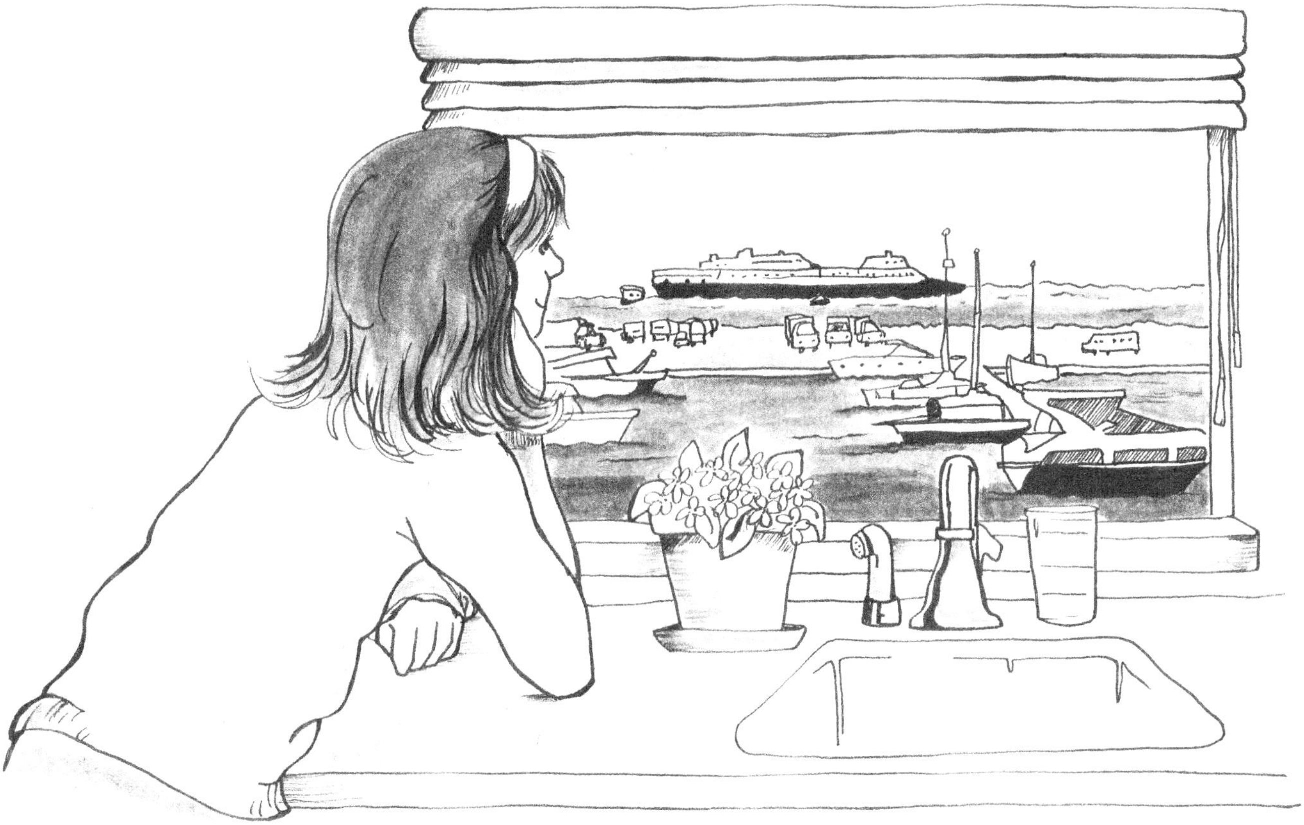

Queen Mary 2
British Isles and Liverpool Salute
World Class
Travel Agent
Fun and Sun
Canada
Japan
Tour
Cruise

# Visit to Town

Aunt Charlotte and Uncle Don enjoy Mary Lou's visit every year. They are delighted by Mary Lou's interest in the big cruise liners that dock across the bay from their house. They also know how children daydream about things.

The next morning Mary Lou is ready to go to town with Aunt Charlotte and Uncle Don. She can hardly wait to get her hands on the information about the big ships.

As they promised, her Aunt and Uncle take Mary Lou to the travel agent's shop. Mary Lou carefully chooses her booklets of information about the Cunard Line ship, the Queen Mary 2. She also selects some brochures about the ports the ship visits.

Mary Lou's parents will be coming to visit Aunt Charlotte and Uncle Don in a few days. She wants to have all the information about the QM2 so she can talk to her parents about the big ship across the harbor.

The travel publications will provide Mary Lou with the facts about the interior of the ship. She will also learn about the activities available on board as well as the ports to be visited.

Mary Lou is hoping that she can convince her parents to take a family cruise on the Queen Mary 2.

# The Parents' Visit

Mary Lou's parents arrive at her Aunt and Uncle's house. They will spend a few days visiting before leaving for their trip home.

Mary Lou has read her QM2 cruise information. That evening at dinner, she begins to tell her parents about the Cunard ships that dock across the harbor. She describes them as having black hulls and red smoke chimneys.

She is so excited! She wants her parents to look out the kitchen window to see the ships lined up in the port.

She tells her parents she has read some travel information about the QM2. She has learned that the ship can hold 2,620 passengers and a crew of 1,250. She explains that the ship is built of steel and is known as an ocean liner.

The QM2 was built for transatlantic service and therefore was designed differently from many other passenger ships. She is the seventh largest cruise ship in the world. The ship's registry is the British Crown colony of Bermuda.

Mary Lou's parents are pleased with all the information she has learned from the travel brochures. They surprise Mary Lou after dinner with the announcement that they plan to take her on a cruise on the QM2 as soon as the school term ends.

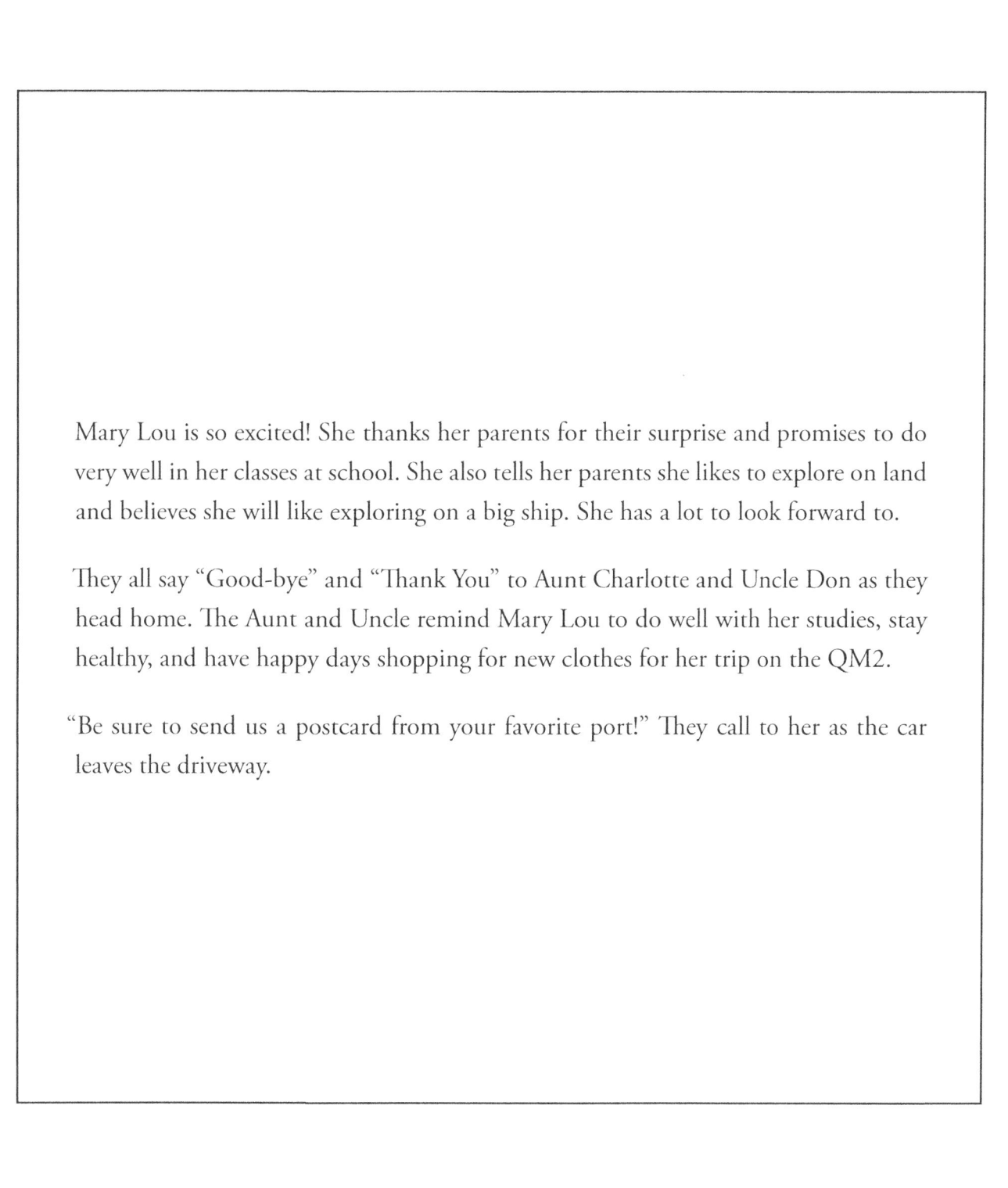

Mary Lou is so excited! She thanks her parents for their surprise and promises to do very well in her classes at school. She also tells her parents she likes to explore on land and believes she will like exploring on a big ship. She has a lot to look forward to.

They all say "Good-bye" and "Thank You" to Aunt Charlotte and Uncle Don as they head home. The Aunt and Uncle remind Mary Lou to do well with her studies, stay healthy, and have happy days shopping for new clothes for her trip on the QM2.

"Be sure to send us a postcard from your favorite port!" They call to her as the car leaves the driveway.

# The Cruise Date Arrives

The big day has arrived! The family will be going on board the Queen Mary 2 in Southampton, England for their ten day roundtrip cruise.

They check-in their suitcases which will be delivered to their assigned room. They continue to get an identification card for the ship. This will be needed to get back on board the ship once they leave the ship for a tour. Mary Lou is so excited to be boarding her favorite ship.

The stateroom she will share with her parents is on Deck 9. It is a lovely, large room with a balcony. Mary Lou cannot believe her luck! The stateroom has a balcony where she can step outside and see the scenery. She can sit on her balcony and look over the land as the ship docks in ports. She is so happy!

# Lifeboat Drill

Mary Lou and her parents have a lifeboat drill as soon as the QM2 leaves Southampton, England. It appears to be disorderly as everyone has to have a life jacket. The life jacket is a buoyant jacket for keeping a person afloat in the water. This jacket will be in the stateroom and there will be one for each person in the room. All passengers are then to report to an assigned lifeboat station. Here they will put on the jacket. It is a practice drill in case there is a ship's emergency.

Mary Lou finds it quite exciting! She does pay attention to the ship officer's directions. She also tries to watch some of the other passengers struggle with their life jackets. She wants to be sure she gets it right the first time. She believes in being prepared.

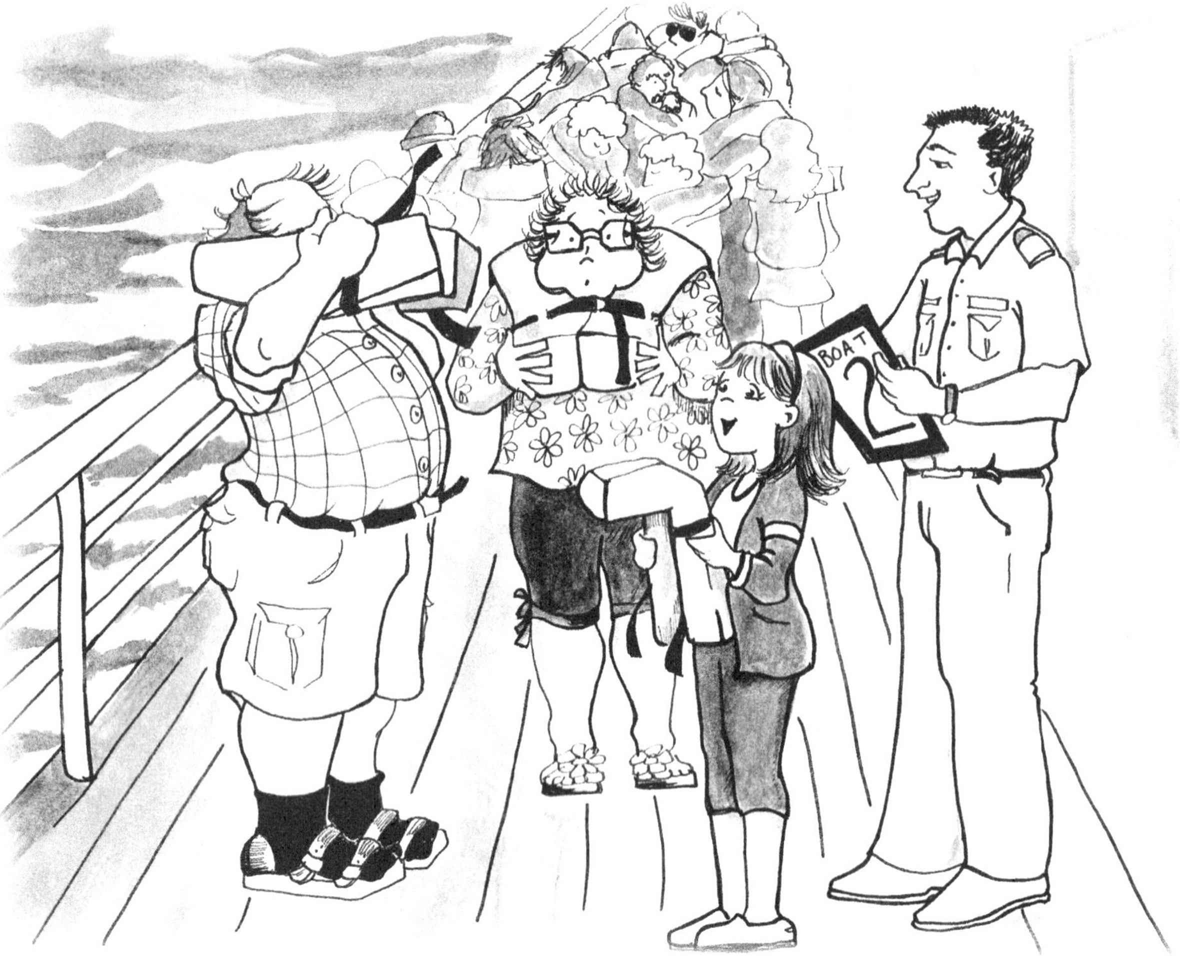
BOAT
2

# Kings Court Buffet

Mary Lou and her parents are so exhausted from the day's activities that they decide to go to an informal dinner for the first night on board the ship.

They go to a giant buffet at Kings Court. There are all types of meals one can choose to eat. This is casual dining at its best!

As they are enjoying their dinners, the family looks over the ship's itinerary of the ports of call. They study the activity sheets which explain what is offered in each port. They will need to make reservations for the excursions they choose before the ship arrives in the port.

# Third Officer Ireson

While they are eating, Mary Lou asks one of the servers about the man in the white uniform. He seems to be checking on all the servers.

The server, Karen, explains that he is a ship's officer. She tells Mary Lou that he is a third officer and his name is Orrin Ireson.

Mary Lou decides she will speak to this officer. She thinks that maybe he can tell her about the ship. She wants to learn all she can about the QM2.

Third Officer Ireson is surprised when a young girl comes up to him to ask him if he can take her on a tour of the ship. She wants to learn all about the ship and how it is driven.

The officer explains to Mary Lou that some parts of the ship are reserved for the crew and the officers. He tells her that any dangerous areas like the engine room and the kitchen areas are restricted.

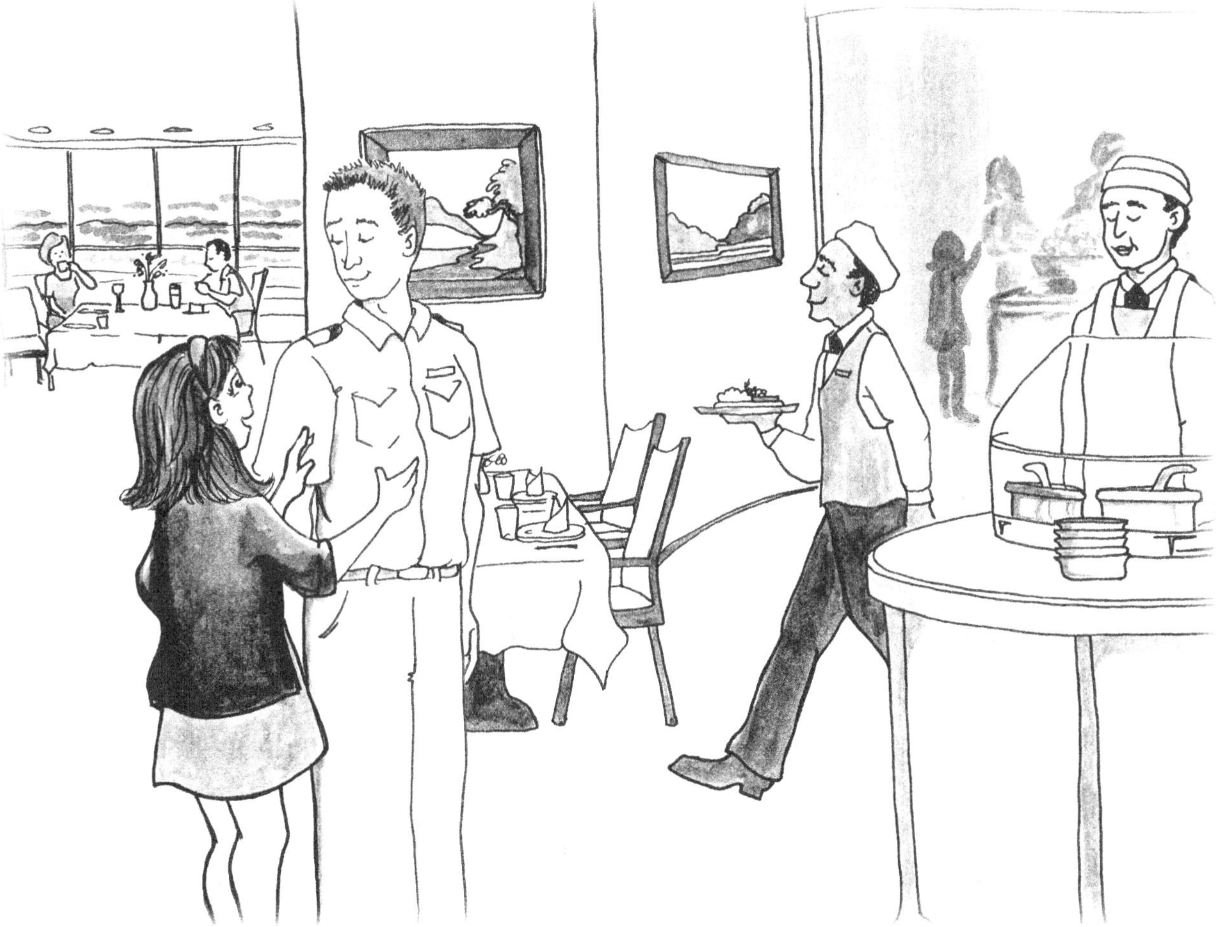

Mary Lou continues to talk to him. She tells him she wants to know about the QM2 because it has always been her dream to sail on this big ocean liner.

She shares with him that she has watched the ship dock in Southampton while she was visiting her Aunt and Uncle in Hythe. She also tells him about sailing past the ship in her Aunt and Uncle's sailboat.

Officer Ireson is pleased with the young girl's interest in exploring the ship. He says to Mary Lou, "Give me your name and stateroom number and tomorrow I will take you on a tour exploring the ship."

Mary Lou runs back to her table. She tells her parents about meeting a ship's officer who will show her around her favorite ship. Her parents know Mary Lou has a strong will. They are not surprised that their daughter made a request to a ship's officer to take her on a tour of the QM2.

# Daily Programme

One of the wonderful things about cruising with Cunard is the Daily Programme. It is in your mailbox outside your stateroom every morning.

Listed in the first copy you receive are all the Senior Officers' names. The department for each one is also listed. So, if you need assistance of any kind you just have to look at the list of departments and the person's name will be printed there.

The Daily Programme will list the ports and the ship's activities for the day. It will list what the entertainment will be in the theater that evening. It will also list the proper attire to wear for the evening hours.

Mary Lou just loves The Daily Programme. She looks at it while having breakfast every morning.

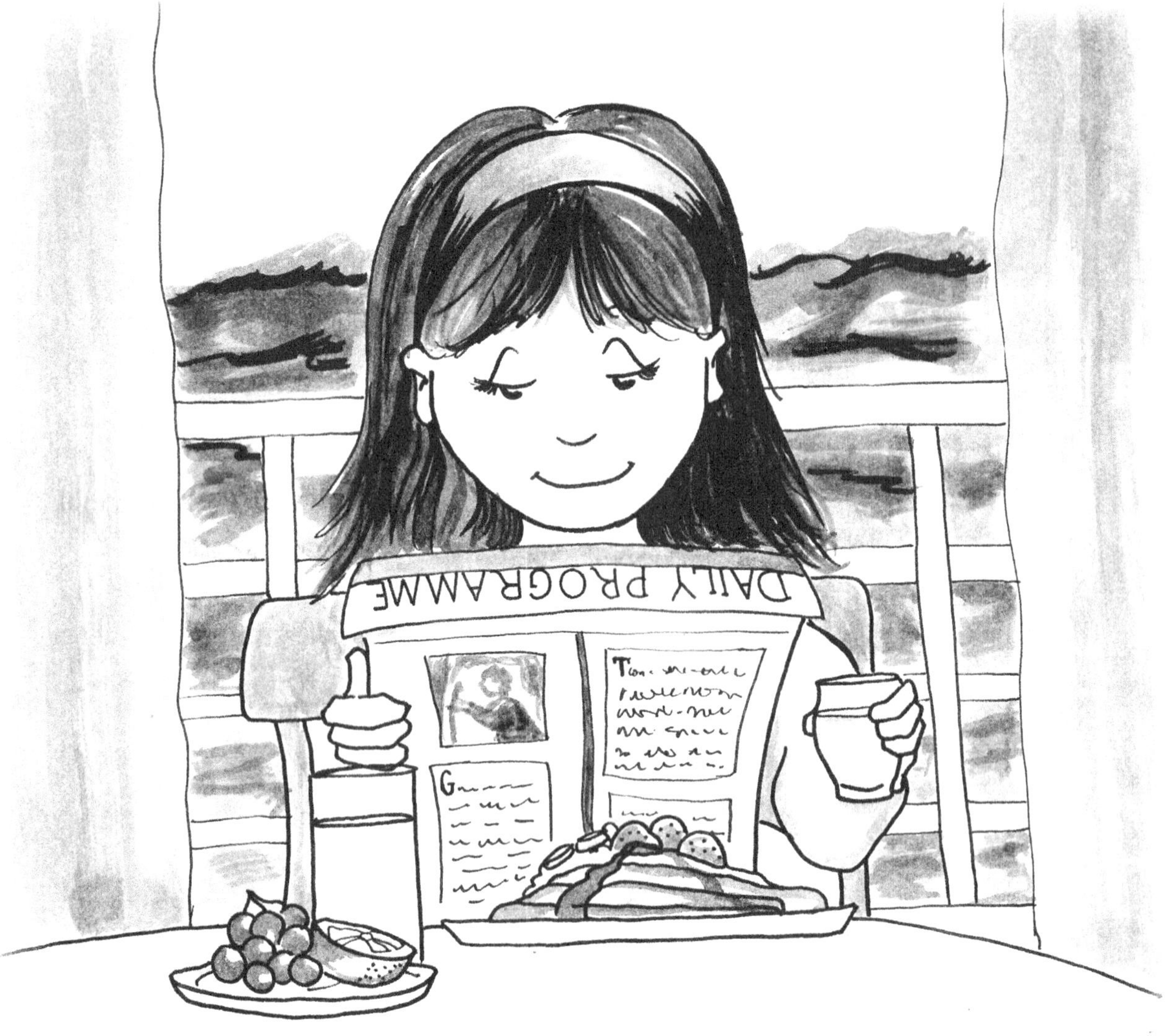
DAILY PROGRAMME

# Breakfast in the Ship's Formal Dining Room

The family awakens in the morning and gets dressed for breakfast in the dining room. This room is called the Britannia Restaurant. Mary Lou learns the dining room is open for breakfast, lunch, and dinner. It is more formal than the upper deck buffet. They order from the menu and are served their breakfasts.

At night, everyone must dress in proper clothing to be seated. Passengers are assigned a table for dinner in the evening. Other evening dining experiences are offered at specialty restaurants for those who wish a different dining menu.

# The Invitation

As they return to the stateroom from breakfast they find a note in the mailbox outside their door. It is from Third Officer Ireson. The note is for Mary Lou. It invites her and her parents to meet him this afternoon in the Grand Lobby on Deck 2 at two o'clock. He will take them on a tour of the ship.

Her parents are thrilled. This is a day at sea. The ship will not be going into any port today. It will be a perfect day to explore the ship with an escort.

Third Officer Ireson is in the Grand Lobby in full white uniform. He is pleased to see Mary Lou with her parents. In fact, he is very pleased to meet the parents of this young girl who is so interested in ships.

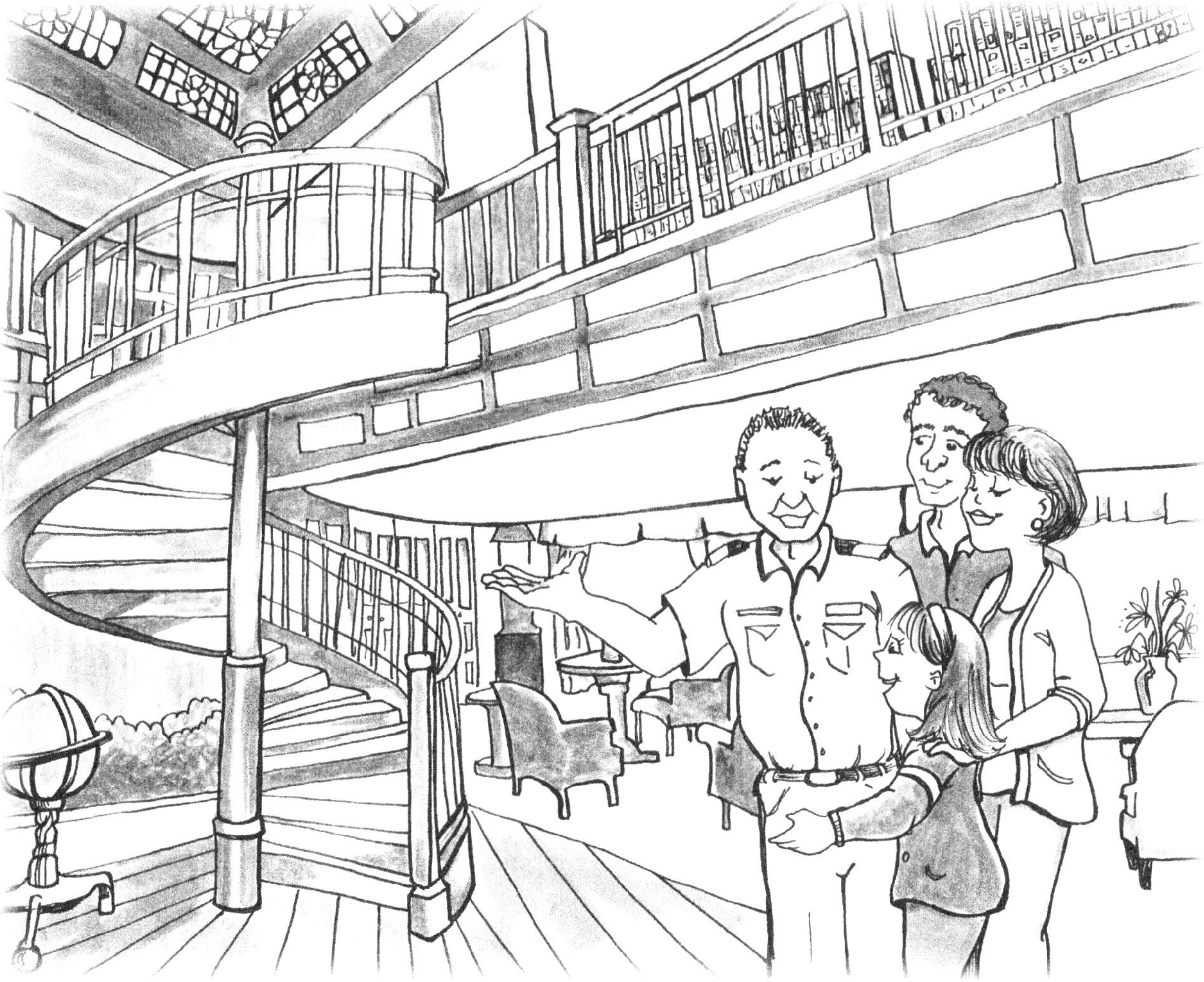

Officer Ireson gives them a wonderful tour of all the decks and facilities of the ship. He even allows them a peek at the main kitchen since it is between meals and no one is dining.

They then all admire the extensive artwork in the gallery as well as the book collection in the library. On one deck they even find some shops. Next they visit the theater and the sports facilities including the large pool.

They learn that there are seventeen decks on board the QM2. However, Mary Lou knows she won't be visiting all those decks. Some are staterooms for the passengers. Some are for other purposes such as sports, the doctor's office and the nurse's room, and other ship business offices.

# Patrick O'Shaughnessy

Mary Lou is still interested to learn how they steer and drive the ship. She asks Officer Ireson,

"How does the Captain know what direction the ship is going?"

Officer Ireson explains,

"The bridge, where this question can be answered, is off limits to all but the ship's personnel."

Mary Lou pleads with Officer Ireson to see that area. The Officer cannot promise such permission would be granted. Only the Captain of the ship can give permission for that tour.

Mary Lou remembers the Captain of the ship making the announcements in the morning for all the passengers. She also remembers that he mentions Patrick O'Shaughnessy as the magical, mystical person who leaves messages for the passengers.

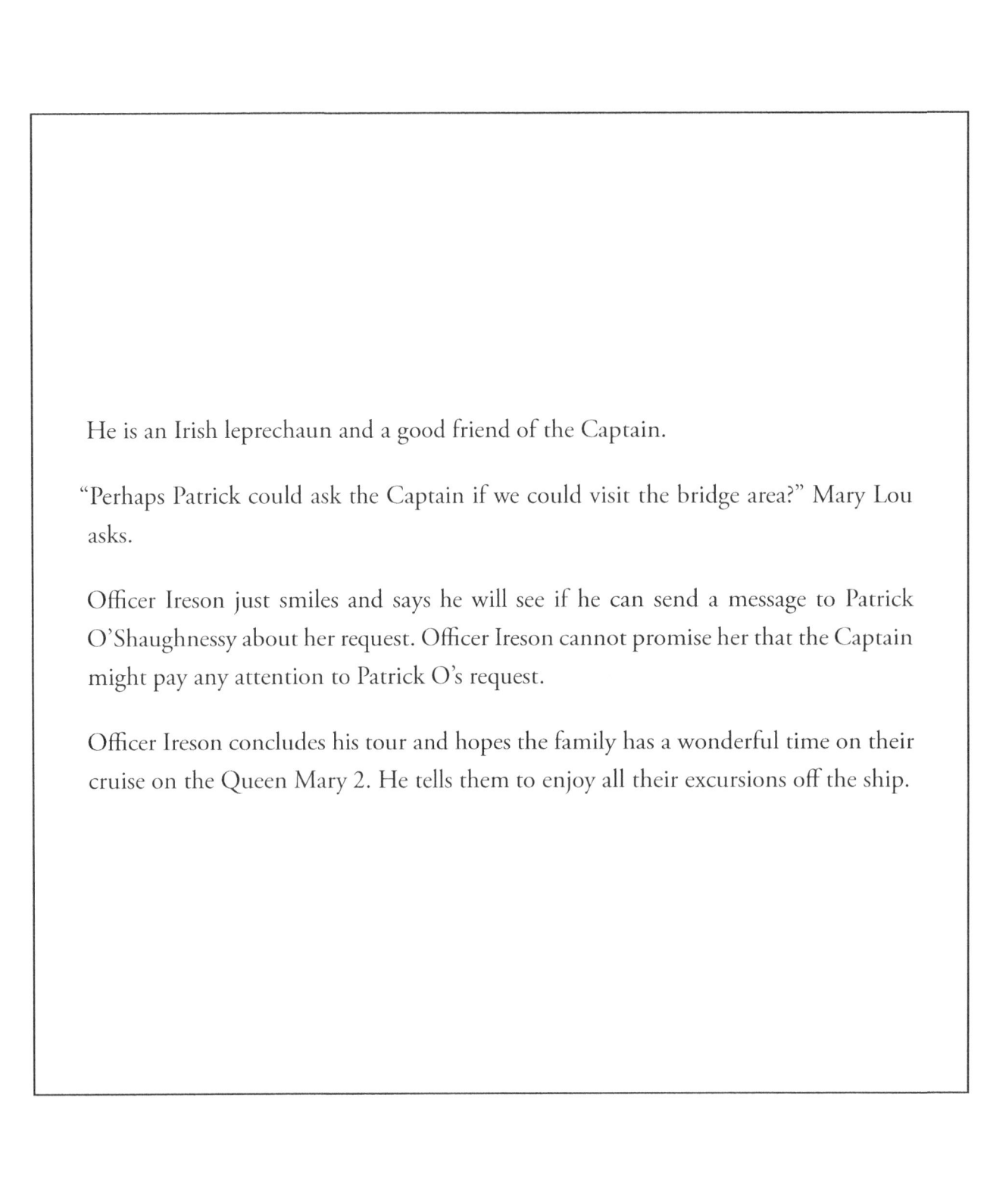

He is an Irish leprechaun and a good friend of the Captain.

"Perhaps Patrick could ask the Captain if we could visit the bridge area?" Mary Lou asks.

Officer Ireson just smiles and says he will see if he can send a message to Patrick O'Shaughnessy about her request. Officer Ireson cannot promise her that the Captain might pay any attention to Patrick O's request.

Officer Ireson concludes his tour and hopes the family has a wonderful time on their cruise on the Queen Mary 2. He tells them to enjoy all their excursions off the ship.

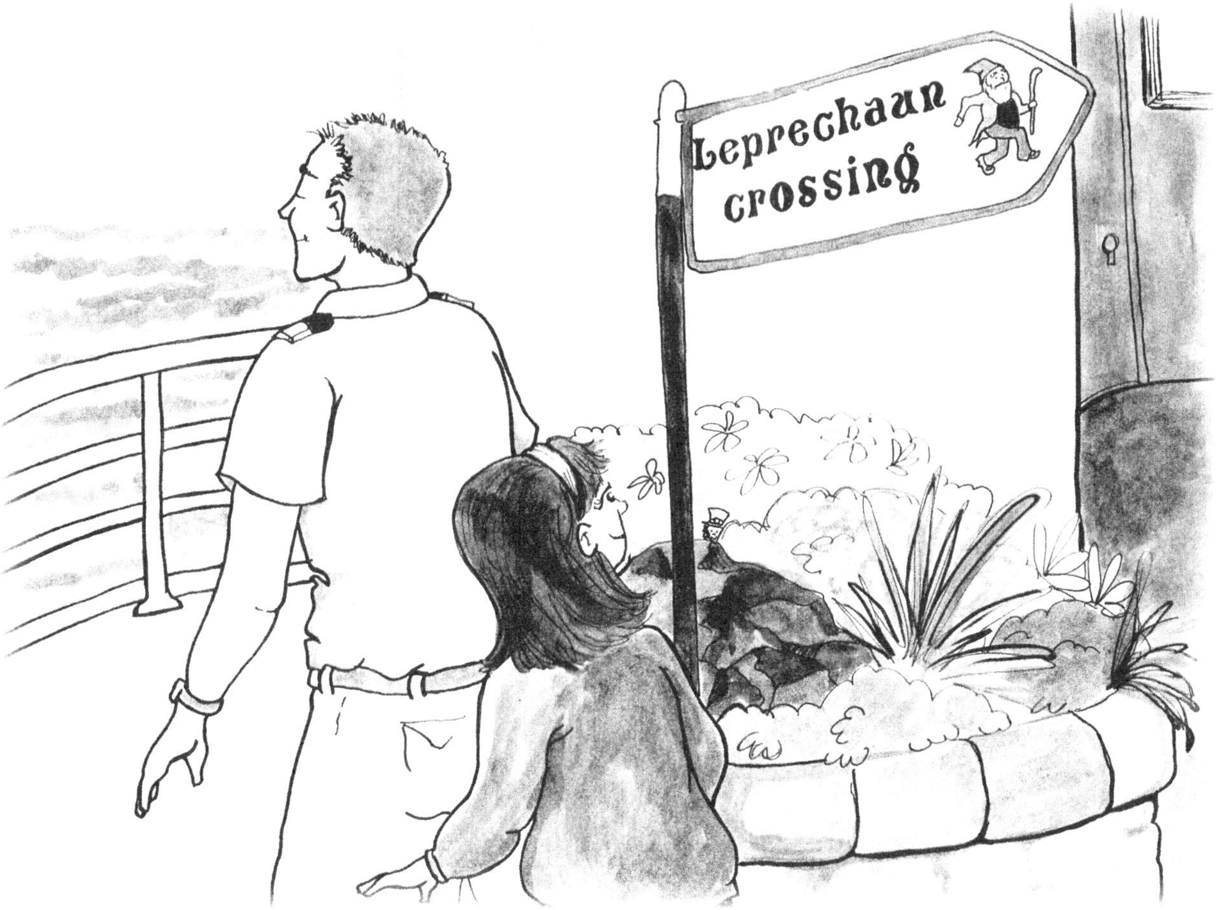
Leprechaun
crossing

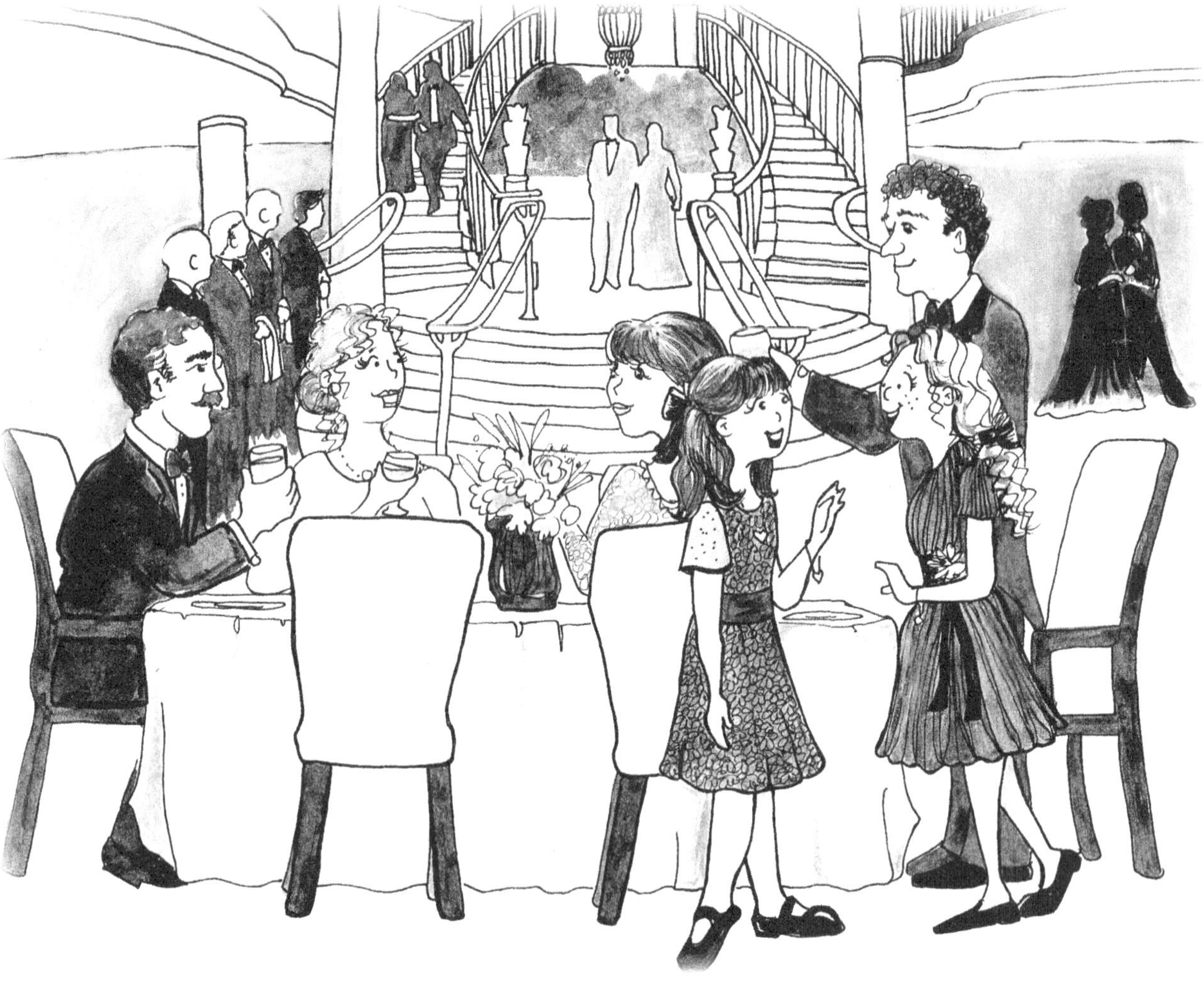

# The First Formal Evening Dinner

It has been a long day! Mary Lou and her parents are looking forward to a lovely dinner.

They return to their stateroom and dress for dinner. Mary Lou is going to wear her new print dress that has a black velvet belt. She will wear her black patent leather shoes. She will place a black velvet bow in her hair. Her mother lets her wear one of her gold chains around her neck.

Mary Lou admires herself in the mirror. She is looking forward to showing off her new clothes to the people at the dining table.

Her father and mother are well dressed. They all go to the Britannia Restaurant dining room for dinner. They are greeted by the maître d' and then shown to their assigned table.

At the table, Mary Lou's father, George Ingham, introduces his family to the other family who will be dining with them.

"Good evening, we are the Ingham family. This is my wife, Jennifer, and my daughter, Mary Lou, and my name is George."

At this time, the other gentleman spoke and introduced his family.

"We are the Smythe family. I am Roger and this is my wife, Evelyn, and my daughter, Rebecca. We are from a village in northern England."

Mary Lou is thrilled to see a young girl about her age seated at the table. She has someone to talk to at dinner while the two sets of parents chat.

The dinner menu is delicious! The passengers each select one of three main dinners and one dessert.

The two families chat together all during dinner. Mary Lou and Rebecca are finding it easy to be together.

# A Routine Begins

Mary Lou records her adventures in her journal each night:

"We have developed a little routine of activity. After our day's tour, we have dinner with our table mates. It's always fun to discuss our trips. The Smythes and their daughter, Rebecca, have taken different tours. We get to talk about each of our experiences on shore."

"After the dinner, both families go to the theater for the special evening show. Exciting acts that include singers and dancers perform. We plan to go to the theater every night. That is why we have selected the early seating for dinner."

"Rebecca and I will plan the next day's free time. We will meet to go to the pool and go swimming. Mrs. Smythe promises to meet us there. Children must have a chaperone with them at the pool. There are no lifeguards. It is so nice to have a friend to do things with when we are not on tours."

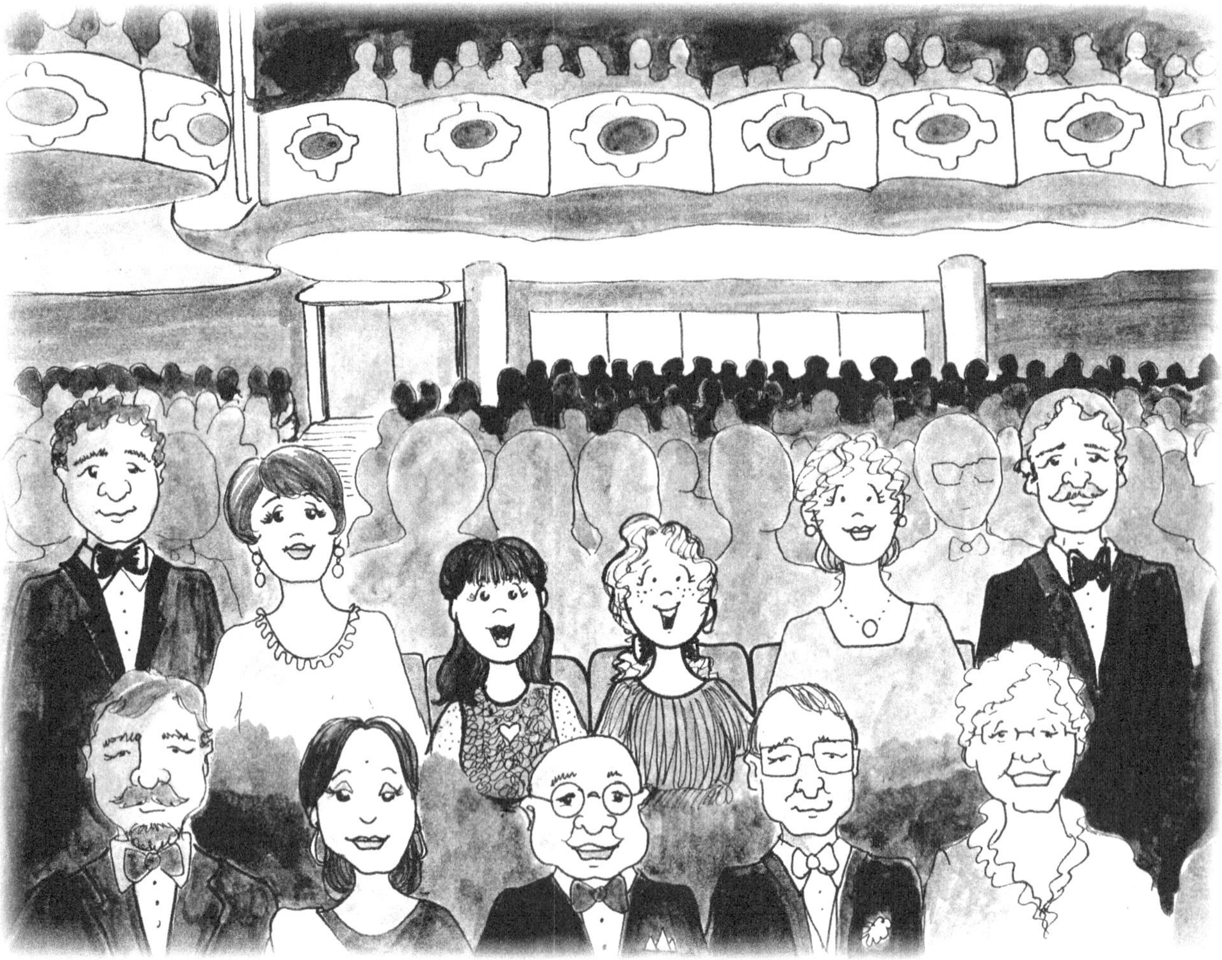

# Selection of Tours

Mary Lou's parents prepare for the tour the three of them will take in the port they will visit the next day.

The family's first tour will be Cork, Ireland. They plan to visit the University College, which is Ireland's most famous college. It has a beautiful campus and is a ten minute walk from the center of the city of Cork.

Nearby Ballycotten is a fishing village and the Cliff Walk is a good way to see the coastal scenery.

Local play, dance and music performances are held in June. This is called Cork Midsummer Festival.

# Day's Plans

Mary Lou's next journal entry:

"The next port we shall visit will be Dublin, Ireland. We will be able to take the Dublin City 'Hop On Hop Off' tour. This tour allows us to get off the bus when we see something we'd like to visit."

"We already have studied the Dublin list of places so we know what we want to see. We have decided on O'Connell Street for shopping; Trinity College to see the famous Book of Kells, which was written by Irish monks in the year 800 A.D.; St. Patrick's Cathedral, which was built to honor the patron Saint of Ireland; Dublin Castle, where the Presidential Inaugurations and State Functions are held; and the last thing we'd like to do is take the boat cruise on the River Liffey. Then we'll see the Ha'penny Bridge."

Mary Lou thinks this sounds like an exciting tour and is looking forward to the day's plans.

# Invitation to the Bridge

One evening after the musical show in the theater, the family returns to their stateroom to find an envelope in their mailbox. It is addressed to Mary Lou and her parents.

Mary Lou opens the note. She discovers that it is an invitation from the Captain and Patrick O'Shaughnessy to visit the ship's navigation bridge. She will learn how the QM2 navigates through the water.

"What a thrill! We are going to see how the ship is driven in the ocean!" exclaims Mary Lou.

Mary Lou's sleep that night is full of dreams about meeting the Captain. She is so looking forward to her visit to the ship's navigation center. She wants to learn how they drive the ship in all kinds of weather.

She sleeps soundly with visions of leprechauns all through the night.

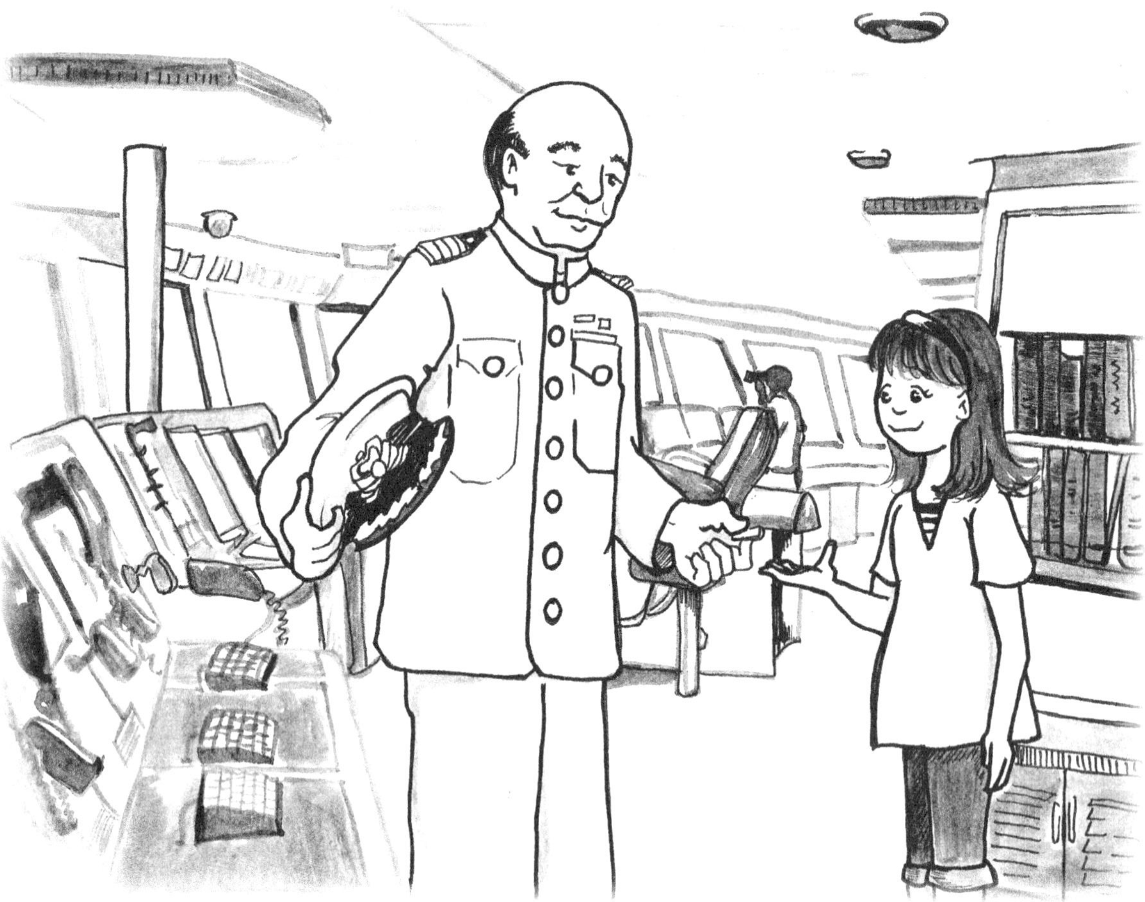

# Visit to the Bridge

Mary Lou and her parents are taken to the Bridge by Officer Ireson to meet the Captain. The Captain will escort them while explaining the Bridge area.

Mary Lou will finally see how a large ship is driven over, or through, the ocean.

Mary Lou is surprised to see so much computer technology. Mary Lou is familiar with seeing the little yachts in the harbor with steering wheels. There are directional screens here which are used to change directions. There are no steering wheels. Radar screens show if anything is near the ship even when it is dark outside. The sailors assigned to the Bridge monitor everything with computer screens.

Mary Lou asks the Captain to explain how he maps out the route they are taking. He shows her the charts that are on the computer screens.

Mary Lou and her parents are so pleased to have had the opportunity to see how the ship sails over the oceans.

The Captain gives Mary Lou a special leprechaun pin of Patrick O'Shaughnessy to remember her visit to the Bridge.

They smile at each other knowing they each share a secret. Mary Lou is filled with joy!

# Continued Sailing and Touring

Mary Lou records her offshore tours in her journal:

"Our stop today will be Glasgow, Scotland which is the largest city in Scotland. It is a city of culture. It has a museum, art galleries, the Theatre Royal, shopping, Victorian architecture and it is the home of the Scottish Opera and Ballet."

"Tomorrow, our port will be Oban, Scotland. This city is a big hub on the west coast of Scotland. It provides access to the Inner and Outer Hebrides Islands. One can take a boat tour from here to the Western Isles, where they have scenery and wildlife tours."

"Then we sail to Liverpool, England. My parents are all excited about visiting this city. It is the home of the famous musical group called The Beatles. I do not know much about them, but I will learn more when I visit the Beatles Museum."

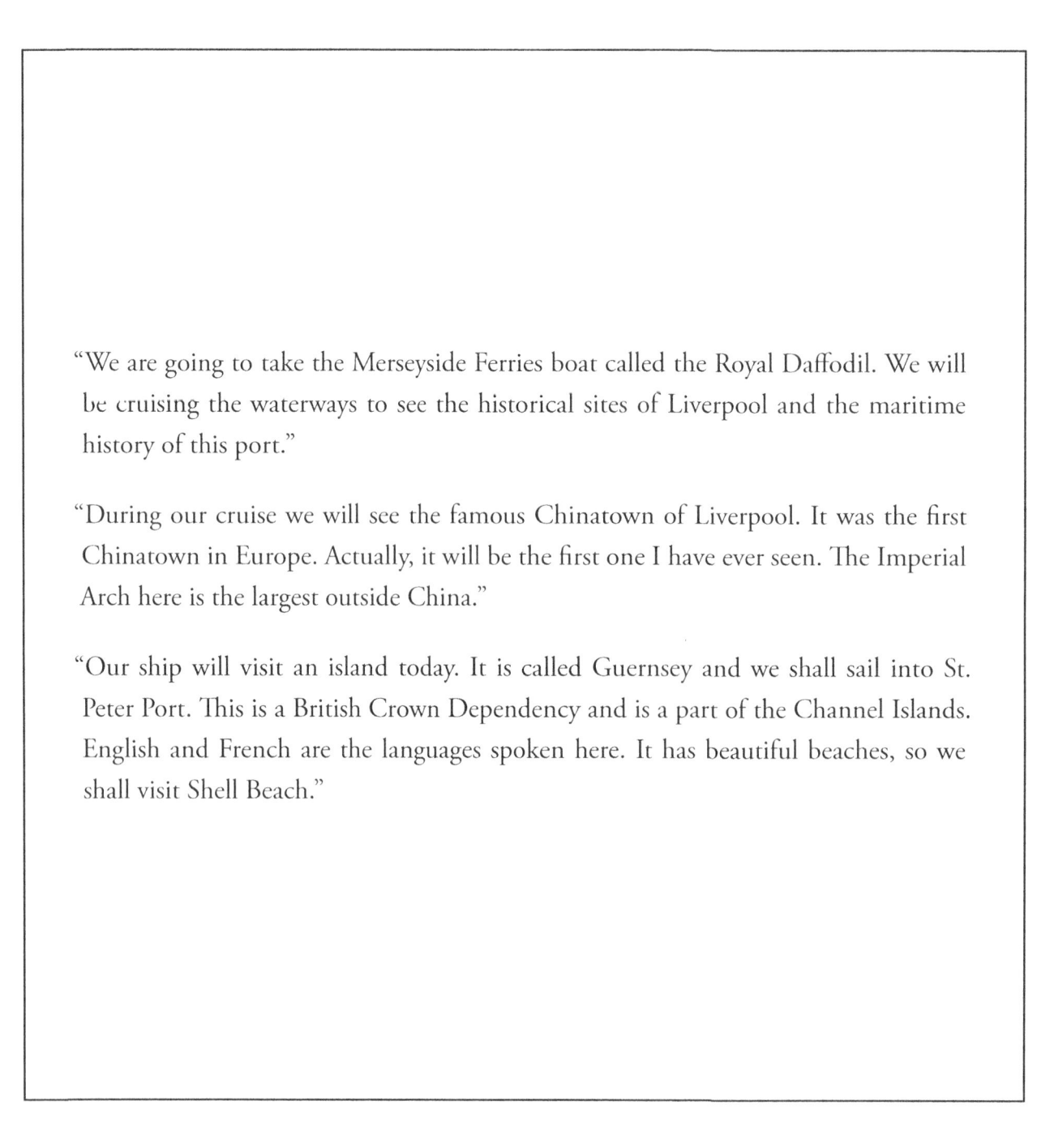

"We are going to take the Merseyside Ferries boat called the Royal Daffodil. We will be cruising the waterways to see the historical sites of Liverpool and the maritime history of this port."

"During our cruise we will see the famous Chinatown of Liverpool. It was the first Chinatown in Europe. Actually, it will be the first one I have ever seen. The Imperial Arch here is the largest outside China."

"Our ship will visit an island today. It is called Guernsey and we shall sail into St. Peter Port. This is a British Crown Dependency and is a part of the Channel Islands. English and French are the languages spoken here. It has beautiful beaches, so we shall visit Shell Beach."

"Our ship will visit an island today."

# Review of Excursions

Dinner is always a much enjoyed time because Mary Lou and her parents meet their table mates, the Smythes. During their dinner everyone discusses the different tours and activities that each family has experienced.

Mary Lou and Rebecca enjoy their evening meal chats. They talk about the things they have seen and the other young people they have met. They have fun playing shuffleboard with a teen group from New York. Their parents are often discussing things they have learned including some of the politics of the country.

Sometimes Rebecca and Mary Lou enjoy evening walks on the Promenade while the parents take a chance at the gaming tables after the theater shows.

# Mary Lou's Last Night on the QM2

Mary Lou makes her final entry in her journal:

"I cannot believe this is the last night of our cruise! I have visited some interesting places. It does not seem possible that ten days could pass so quickly. I am looking forward to having my final breakfast in the dining room tomorrow. I shall say 'Good-bye' to all the wait staff."

"I must buy a few more souvenirs of the ship to take back to my friends. I am going to buy some bookmarks with Queen Mary 2 printed on them. I'll also buy some postcards with pictures of the ship. I want to add them to my real photos for the album I plan to make of my cruise."

"I am going to buy something for Rebecca, my new friend. I will give it to her tomorrow when we exchange addresses. We plan to stay in touch and perhaps visit each other."

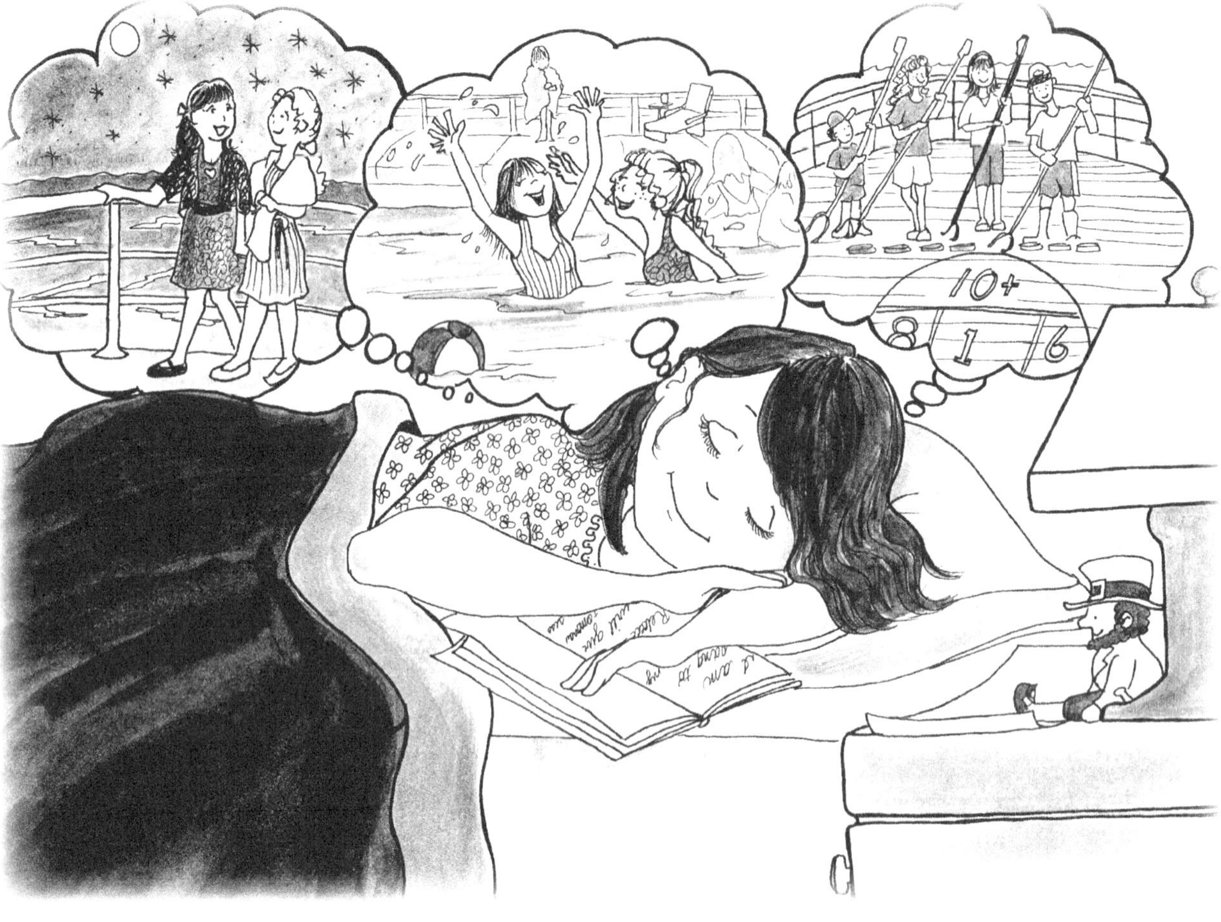
10+
8
1
6

# Mary Lou's Thoughts on Her Cruise

As Mary Lou closes her eyes and drifts off to sleep on her last night on the Queen Mary 2, she thinks about how fantastic this cruise has been.

The ship offered all the traditional charm of an ocean liner: English afternoon tea was available, the ship's décor was beautiful and guests dressed for dinner.

Mary Lou will always remember the great games of shuffleboard she and Rebecca played with the other young people on board from America and England. What fun it was! They also had some great walks on the Promenade where they enjoyed watching the activities and dress of the different passengers.

Now she will be returning to Southampton, England. The family will spend a few days in Hythe Marina Village with her Aunt Charlotte and Uncle Don before they return home to their daily lives and activities in their little village. She is looking forward to telling them about her cruise and all the places they visited.

She will also tell them about the mystical Patrick O'Shaughnessy who lives aboard the Queen Mary 2.

## The End

Author Joan J. Curley had two desires: to travel and to write. Her writing was put on hold while her attention was given to her life career as an educator, elementary teacher, school counselor K-12, and school principal. However, the travel continued.

She circumnavigated the world twice. Joan lived in England and she and her husband, Neil, lived and worked in Massachusetts, Bermuda, Guam, Germany, and Egypt. Joan was born in Massachusetts and earned a Bachelor's degree from Newton College of the Sacred Heart, a Master's degree from Boston University and completed numerous post-graduate courses on Administrations, Counseling, and Educational Law at Salem State College, Tufts University and the University of Guam. She also studied at Julius Maximilian University of Wurzburg, Germany. After retiring from her educational career of thirty-nine years, Joan decided to turn her attention to writing. She wanted to share her life and career experiences in stories for children. Joan believes that a children's book with a story could be a stimulus for parents and teachers to encourage children to improve their writing skills. This would help children to be more successful in their school studies.

Joan has published eight other children's books. Each book is based on what she has observed in places where she has lived and worked. An avid traveler, she hopes her stories encourage children to explore new interests and learn new information that is available to all in our technological society.

Joan is an active member of her Naples, Florida community. She is a member of the Collier County Republican Executive Committee, Naples Press Club (former President), Sandollars Club, East Naples Civic Association, Women's Republican Club of Naples Federated, and the Naples Art Association.

Joan has received numerous awards including: Woman of the Year Award from the Business and Professional Women's Club of Massachusetts; a commission from the governor of Guam to become a member of the Ancient Order of the Chamorri (a distinguished award for service to the people of Guam); and Minister of Education recognition for educational service in Bermuda.

## BOOKS BY JOAN J. CURLEY

*Tanika and the Kiskadee*
(Bermuda)

*Tarek and the Talking Egyptian Horns*
(Cairo, Egypt)

*All Boats Have Pretzels*
(Martha's Vineyard)

*Hi, My Name is Keiko*
(Japan)

*Lily, The Orphan Hen*
(Guam)

*Lucian's Boat*
(New England Coast)

*The Dandelion Slayers*
(Martha's Vineyard)

*Malcolm, the Muscovy Duck of Naples, Florida*
(Naples, Florida)

Made in the USA
Coppell, TX
26 May 2025